Contents

Words that appear in **bold** can be found in the glossary on page 30.

The Geography Detective, Sherlock Bones, will help you learn all about National Parks and Conservation Areas. The answers to Sherlock's questions can be found on page 31.

What are national parks and conservation areas?

Conservation is the protection of wild places, plants and animals. Conservation can also be about preserving historic buildings, or even a group of people and their way of life. National parks and conservation areas are special places that have been set aside to protect nature and also so that people can enjoy the outdoors.

National parks and conservation areas are usually wild places that are run and often owned by the country's government. **Development** in these places is carefully controlled, and **pollution** is kept to a minimum, so that much of the area is natural and unspoiled. National parks often contain spectacular scenery, such as high, craggy mountains, dense forests and rugged coastlines. Many conservation areas contain rare plants and animals.

DETECTIVE WORK

Find out about the largest national park in your country. How big is it? Why is it special?

In Australia, the Uluru-Kata Tjuta National Park was set up in the 1950s to protect the landscape and also the local Aboriginal people and their culture. The park includes the world's largest rock, Uluru, which is sacred to the Aboriginals.

Conservation areas vary a lot in size. Some national parks are huge, and the very biggest are the size of small countries. Some nature reserves are tiny – for example, a small patch of woodland on the edge of a city. There are over 6,500 protected areas worldwide, covering over a million square km – 12 per cent of Earth's surface. Conservation areas are found on every continent, including Antarctica, which is in fact one huge, icy wildlife reserve.

National parks vary in character as well as size. In places such as North America, they are vast wilderness areas where very few people live, and which may receive relatively few visitors. Others are home to thousands of people. The most popular receive millions of visitors. Large numbers of people can cause problems for nature, so the authorities have to work hard to prevent damage to the natural world.

FOCUS ON

The world's largest parks and reserves

The world's largest national park is Northeast Greenland National Park. Covering 972,000 sq km, it is roughly the size of Egypt and was set up in 1974. The whole of Antarctica is a protected area, where mining and other development is not permitted. However, because no one country owns Antarctica, it is not a national park, but a protected site instead.

Mining and other development has been banned in Antarctica since 1998. The seas around the continent are a marine sanctuary.

Why do we need national parks and conservation areas?

The planet we live on has many different **habitats**, such as rainforests, deserts and grasslands. Each is home to particular types of plants and animals. However, the growing numbers of people on Earth are putting pressure on these wild places. National parks and other conservation areas are set up to protect wild places from development.

Plants and animals living in a certain habitat are suited to the particular conditions found there. For example, a tiger living in a rainforest would not survive in the Arctic, while polar bears from the Arctic would not survive in a rainforest. However, as the number of people on Earth has risen pressure on space has increased, so more and more wild habitats have been destroyed or altered. This is called **habitat loss**.

In the last century or so, large areas of the world's rainforests, like this one in Borneo, have been cut down for timber or to create new farmland.

DETECTIVE WORK

Find out about the different habitats in your nearest national park. What types of wildlife are found there? Are there rare species? Try logging onto the park website or looking at park leaflets.

Since the early 1800s, the world's human **population** has risen from one billion to over 6.5 billion. All over the world, towns and cities have grown rapidly to provide homes for everyone. Wild areas such as forests and grasslands have been destroyed to create farmland to grow all the food people need. Other wild land has been swallowed up by mines, factories, roads and other developments.

Tigers are now scarce because so many have been hunted for their fur. They are also killed because they are thought to be dangerous. Some of the forests where they live have been felled.

FOCUS ON

Hunting and collecting

Habitat loss is not the only threat to the world's wildlife. For centuries, many types of animals have been hunted for food, and also for their hides and other body parts. Elephants and rhinos are killed for their valuable tusks or horns. In 1900 there were about 10 million African elephants, now only about 600,000 are left.

When wild habitats are taken over by people, the plants and animals that live there are put at risk. Some **species** have become **extinct** – have died out altogether. Luckily, in the last century or so, more and more people have realised that we have a duty to protect nature. And the most effective way of doing that is to set aside whole habitats where plants, animals and other wildlife can thrive.

Are there different types of conservation areas?

There are several types of conservation area. National parks are often large areas, containing many different habitats, such as forests, lakes and mountains. Conservation areas such as nature reserves are generally smaller. Some have been set up to protect just a single small habitat, such as unusual woodland, or even a particular type of tree, plant or animal.

Britain has several types of conservation areas. England, Wales and Scotland have 14 national parks, of which Cairngorms National Park in Scotland is the largest, covering 3,800 square kilometres. In addition, there are large protected sites called Areas of Outstanding Natural Beauty, and smaller National Nature Reserves. A conservation area can also protect a historic site or important building.

In Britain, the term national park is a bit misleading. For the most part, these areas are not owned by the nation but by private landowners and farmers, though some land is owned by charities such as the National Trust.

In Britain some conservation areas are known as AONBs. What do you think the initials stand for?

The historic city of Havana on the Caribbean island of Cuba is a World Heritage Site. The buildings here date from the 1500s when Cuba was a Spanish colony.

The term reserve can also be confusing. In the past, game reserves were private parks in places such as Africa, where people hunted big game like lions. Nowadays little hunting goes on, and most of these reserves are run as conservation areas.

National parks and conservation areas are usually looked after by the nation's government. Sometimes international organisations are also involved. In 1975, the United Nations began to establish World Heritage Sites to protect the world's finest scenery and historic places. A total of 878 sites have now been protected in this way. Some are wild places such as mountain ranges, but others are historic buildings, or even whole cities. The pyramids of ancient Egypt, the Statue of Liberty in New York, and the city of Venice, Italy are all World Heritage Sites.

DETECTIVE WORK

Find out about coral reefs using books or the Internet. You could find out more about the Great Barrier Reef at www.cultureand recreation.gov.au/articles/ greatbarrierreef/. Alternatively, find out about marine or coastal reserves in your country.

FOCUS ON

Marine reserves

Not all parks and conservation areas are on dry land! Some protect a large lake or string of lakes. Marine and coastal reserves protect watery habitats such as coral reefs and the wildlife they contain. The Great Barrier Reef stretches for 2,600 kilometres (1,600 miles) off the coast of northeastern Australia. This is the world's longest coral reef and also the largest World Heritage Site.

Coral reefs are one of the richest habitats in the oceans. The Great Barrier Reef is home to hundreds of different fish, molluscs, sponges and shrimps.

How are national parks and conservation areas set up?

Almost every country in the world has conservation areas. However, this wasn't always so. The idea of national parks began in North America in the early 1800s, and the first park was set up there in 1872.

In 1864, President Abraham Lincoln passed a law giving a beautiful wilderness called Yosemite to the state of California 'for public use, resort and **recreation**'. In 1872, the United States established the world's first national park, at Yellowstone in the Rocky Mountains. Other countries soon copied the idea. Australia's first national park was set up in 1879, while Banff, Canada's first park, was established in 1885.

FOCUS ON

Support for new parks

In the 1870s, the creation of Yellowstone National Park was supported by **conservationists**, politicians and also local businesses – notably the North Pacific Railroad which realised a park would mean more custom for the railroad. However, new parks are not always popular. In 1973, plans to set up a park in the Cumbrian Mountains in Wales were scrapped when local landowners opposed the idea.

Yellowstone Park covers 8,983 square km (3,468 square miles) of rugged mountain country with lakes, hot springs and geysers (a special type of hot spring).

Europe's first national parks were established in Sweden in 1908. However other European countries, such as Britain, lagged behind partly because even Britain's wildest places were extensively settled and farmed. In the 1950s, eleven national parks were set up to protect Britain's finest scenery from overdevelopment. Three more have been added since 2003. In the last 50 years or so, national parks and conservation areas have been established all over the world. New sites are added each year. The number of World Heritage Sites has increased rapidly – over 60 new sites were added between 2005 and 2008.

National parks in the United States are managed by the National Park Service, set up in 1916. As well as 58 parks, the service also manages over 330 other protected areas. Britain's national parks are managed by the National Parks Authorities (NPAs), each headed by a committee which includes government officials and local people. For a new national park to be created, the country's government has to pass a law. Studies are carried out and the government, scientists, landowners and local people have to agree it is a good idea.

Cairngorms

Loch Lomond and the Trossachs

Northumberland

North York Moors

Lake District

Yorkshire Dales

Snowdonia

Peak District

Broads Authority

Brecon Beacons

Pembrokeshire Coast

Exmoor

South Downs

New Forest

Dartmoor

 National Park

 Proposed National Park

This map shows Britain's national parks. The South Downs is likely to become a new national park.

Study the map of Britain's national parks. Where are most of the parks found?

What kinds of landscapes can you see in parks and conservation areas?

National parks and other conservation areas contain some of the world's most beautiful and spectacular scenery. Parks around the world have soaring mountain peaks, deep canyons, gushing waterfalls, glittering lakes and rugged coastlines. So how did all these amazing landscapes form?

Many national parks are located in rugged mountain areas. Most mountains are formed by a process called **uplift**, driven by huge forces inside the Earth. Upheaval in the hot, semi-liquid rocks deep underground set the giant, rigid plates that form Earth's outer **crust** in motion. Where two plates very slowly crash together, the border zone crumples upward to form a range of **fold mountains**, such as the European Alps or the Himalayas in Asia. Volcanic eruptions can also form high mountains, such as Mount Kilimanjaro in East Africa.

Most of the other spectacular landscapes seen in national parks have been formed by **erosion** – the gradual wearing away of the land by forces such as running water, wind, frost and ice.

Steep, pyramid-shaped peaks such as the Matterhorn in the Alps in Switzerland were carved by glaciers flowing down the mountain on all sides.

The Grand Canyon measures 1.8 km (over a mile) deep.

FOCUS ON

The Grand Canyon

In western USA, the Colorado River has carved one of the world's deepest canyons, up to 29 km (18 miles) wide and 446 km (277 miles) long. The canyon is located on a high **plateau** created by uplift. Even as the area was uplifted, wind, rain and rushing water carved a deep canyon. The river continues to erode its bed.

The Grand Canyon is still getting a little bit deeper each year. Can you explain why?

Rushing water in rivers and streams can carve wide valleys, sheer gorges and deep **canyons** such as America's Grand Canyon. Where a river flows over a ledge of hard rock a waterfall forms. In areas of limestone rock such as the Yorkshire Dales National Park, water seeping underground can carve caves and channels. On the coast, strong waves eat into the shore to form high cliffs.

Ice erosion has created spectacular scenery in many regions, including Britain. During long, cold periods called **Ice Ages**, ice covered much of Britain. Slow-moving glaciers carved deep, U-shaped valleys. Where ice lingered in hollows it formed lakes. The last Ice Age ended about 10,000 years ago.

DETECTIVE WORK

Find out about the forces of erosion that have shaped the landscape in your nearest national park using the Internet, park leaflets or reference books. Does the park contain rivers and lakes? Are there mountains, and if so, are they snow-covered? Was the area ever covered by ice?

Who lives in national parks and conservation areas?

I n many parts of the world, national parks are mainly wilderness areas where very few people live. Britain's national parks are very different, being home to many thousands of people, and often containing quite large towns.

DETECTIVE WORK

Find out how many people live in your nearest national park using the Internet or your local library. What are the biggest **settlements** there? What are the most important industries?

In New Zealand, only small numbers of hikers are given permits to trek the remote Routeburn Trail.

The Peak District in Derbyshire is one of Britain's most densely populated parks. Around 38,000 people live in the park, which covers 1,437 square km. There are several towns, such as Bakewell. The Lake District has 42,000 people living in 2,292 square km. In other parts of the world, parks that look wild and untouched may be inhabited. The Masai Mara Reserve in Kenya is home to the Masai people, who are traditionally cattle-herders. In North America some parks have very few inhabitants. The Grand Canyon National Park covering 4,931 square km has only about 1,000 people.

You can work out a region's population density by dividing the number of inhabitants by the area (in square kilometres).
Which park is more densely populated, the Peak District or the Lake District?

This aerial view shows the port and oil refineries at Milford Haven.

Pollution

Industry in Britain's national parks can cause pollution. Milford Haven, a major port and oil refinery, is surrounded by the wild coastline of the Pembrokeshire National Park in South Wales. In 1996, an oil tanker ran aground offshore, spilling 72,000 tonnes of oil into the sea. About 100 km (60 miles) of coastline were polluted and thousands of seabirds died.

Where there are people, there must be work. Mining, industry and farming are banned in many national parks. However Britain's national parks include farmland where farmers have grown crops or raised sheep or cattle for centuries. Mining and quarrying are traditional industries in parks in the Peak District and Yorkshire Dales, and there are even factories and power plants. These industries help the local economy, but can cause pollution.

Tourism is an important industry in most national parks. The Peak District, Britain's most popular park, receives about 22 million visitors each year. Many people visit from nearby cities, and the park is also easily reached from motorways. In parks that are true wilderness areas, visitor numbers may be purposefully kept low by charging people a fee to enter the park, and issuing a limited number of permits. This is usually done to minimise harm to the **environment** and protect wildlife.

What are the aims of national parks and conservation areas?

National parks and conservation areas generally have two main aims. The first is to protect the habitats within their borders. The second is to allow people to enjoy the park and learn about nature. These two aims sometimes conflict with one another, which can lead to difficult decisions for the authorities.

The work of rangers

Most parks and conservation areas employ rangers or wardens who look after the day-to-day running of the reserve. Rangers look after habitats and wildlife. They also maintain paths and provide information for visitors, which may include giving talks on local wildlife. They may advise local people such as farmers on conservation.

The main purpose of any conservation area is to protect the environment – the wild scenery and in some cases, historic buildings. National parks are also set up for leisure and recreation. They aim to attract visitors, not least because tourists bring in money, which helps the local economy or funds conservation work.

The work of rangers may include leading walks that explain about nature inside the park. This ranger is showing visitors around Grand Teton national park in the United States.

Large numbers of visitors can damage nature, for example by leaving litter. The authorities must manage visitors so that their presence does not harm the very attractions they come to see.

Ever since the early days of conservation, parks and nature reserves have introduced rules to protect the environment. For example, people are not allowed to pick flowers, damage plants or disturb wildlife. Visitors are often excluded from areas where birds and other animals are breeding. 'Take nothing but photos, leave nothing but footprints' is the general rule.

As well as the main aims of protecting nature and providing a place for recreation, park authorities also manage natural resources such as forests and **minerals**. Again, this has to be done in ways that do not harm nature. In Britain, where national parks have many towns and villages, the authorities also try to protect the interests of local people. This can include providing jobs, for example in forestry, and also in the running of all the services that visitors need.

This area of a beach in Brazil has been fenced off during the turtles' nesting season.

DETECTIVE WORK

Investigate the aims of your nearest national park using the park website or published leaflets. Parks sometimes set out their aims in a 'mission statement'. Find out about the work park rangers do.

How do living things survive in the natural world?

Nature conservation is about protecting all the wildlife in a habitat, including plants, animals, fungi and even tiny living things that are too small to see. All have a part to play in the cycle of life.

Every large habitat, such as a forest, contains many smaller habitats, such as clearings, streams and wooded hillsides. Every living tree and even a dead, mossy stump has its own set of living things, like a miniature world.

The plants, animals and other living things in a habitat depend on each other for food. The relationships between them can be shown in food chains like the one on the right. At the base of the chain are plants, which produce their own food using sunlight energy and minerals. **Herbivores** such as insects, slugs and earthworms feed on plants, and are hunted by animals such as shrews and songbirds. In turn, shrews are eaten by **predators** such as hawks. When living things die, their remains are broken down by insects, fungi and bacteria. Minerals return to the soil to nourish plants, and so the cycle of life begins again.

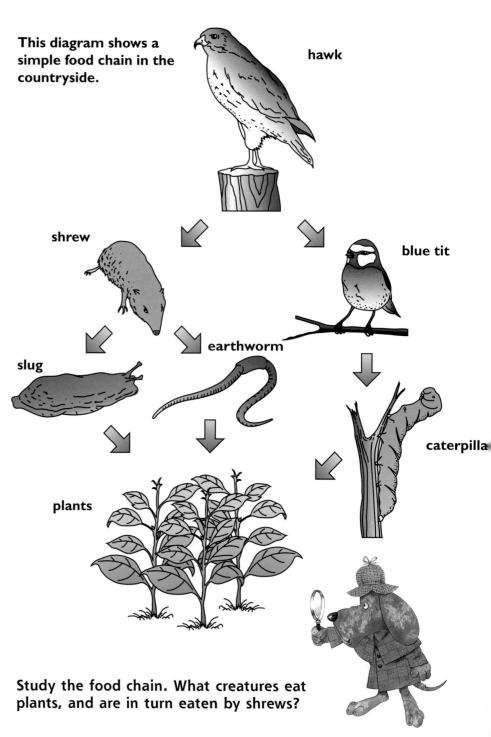

This diagram shows a simple food chain in the countryside.

hawk

shrew

blue tit

slug

earthworm

caterpilla

plants

Study the food chain. What creatures eat plants, and are in turn eaten by shrews?

Feeding habits

Animals that eat many different foods, such as rats and foxes, do well in many different habitats, such as woodlands, farmland and even in towns. Some animals eat only one food. For example, the giant panda eats only bamboo. It thrives only in one particular environment – the remote bamboo forests of China, which are now protected.

DETECTIVE WORK

Make a list of all the mini-habitats you can find in your garden or in a corner of the local park. For example, ponds, piles of logs or stones, hedges and flower beds are all mini-habitats. Make a map of the area showing all the habitats.

Animals with a restricted diet, such as the giant panda, cannot cope if their habitat changes. Flexible feeders such as foxes and rats cope well with change.

Every species in a food chain depends on the next links in the chain for survival. If one link is broken or damaged, the whole chain is affected. For example, farmers sometimes put chemicals on their crops to kill crop-eating insects. If all the insects die, the songbirds that eat them will starve, and the hawks that prey on smaller birds may also die. In national parks, farmers are encouraged not to use chemicals that can harm nature in this way.

How do conservationists protect rare wildlife?

National parks and conservation areas aim to protect all the living things within their boundaries. But sometimes that is not enough. Special action may be needed to save a rare species from extinction. Species that are in serious danger of dying out are called **endangered**.

Many animals that have been hunted for centuries are now rare. For example, leopards and rhinos are very scarce because so many have keen killed for their skins or ivory. Endangered animals such as these are now mostly found in conservation areas. The countries concerned now have strict laws banning hunting, but **poachers** still kill the animals **illegally**. Some reserves where endangered animals live are patrolled by armed guards to keep poachers away.

Conservation on the Galapagos

The remote Galapagos Islands in the eastern Pacific are home to many unique animals, such as giant tortoises and marine iguanas. **Native** species are threatened by new predators such as cats and rats. Goats brought to the islands by sailors have stripped the vegetation. Conservation work includes the painstaking removal of non-native species.

The marine iguana is a rare and unusual reptile found only on the Galapagos Islands.

Nakuru National Park in East Africa, home of the endangered black rhino, is entirely surrounded by an electric fence to keep poachers at bay. Armed wardens patrol the park.

DETECTIVE WORK

Conservation organisations such as the World Wide Fund for Nature and Greenpeace campaign to save endangered species, such as whales, tigers and rhinos, from extinction. Find out more about their work by logging onto their websites (see page 31).

In many parts of the world, native plants and animals are threatened by new species that people have brought to the area either deliberately or by accident. The newcomers are known as **alien species**, and they can be a particular menace in small or confined habitats such as islands. The islands of New Zealand are home to several types of flightless birds. Centuries ago, these vulnerable animals had few predators, but now newcomers such as cats, dogs and rats prey on them and have greatly reduced their numbers.

Endangered animals are put on the Red List of Threatened Species, which is published by the International Union for Conservation of Nature (IUCN). Conservationists acting to save a species from extinction must first find out about its needs, such as the food and the ideal habitat required. Rare birds are ringed, and radio collars are fitted to mammals such as leopards, so scientists can track their movements and learn about their behaviour. Endangered species are sometimes bred in captivity. If the breeding programme is successful, the young animals may later be released in reserves.

How do parks and conservation areas provide for visitors?

National parks encourage people to explore the outdoors. Some people come to spot birds or flowers. As well as traditional pursuits such as walking, camping and fishing, parks now encourage a huge range of activities, such as potholing, white-water rafting, mountain biking and windsurfing. Services provided by the park help people to get the most out of their visit.

These visitors to Denali National Park in Alaska have come across a bear on their bike ride.

In some Asian parks, such as Chitwan National Park, Nepal, elephant safaris give tourists the chance to get close to dangerous wildlife such as tigers and crocodiles.

Most visitors reach national parks by car. Once in the park, however, people are encouraged to leave their car and explore by other means, including on foot, horseback or bicycle. Some visitors take to the air in hang-gliders or hot-air balloons. In parks with lakes or by the sea, swimming, sailing, canoeing, snorkelling or diving may be popular.

Park authorities work hard to provide all the services people need, from cafés and car parks to information centres. Many people visit only for the day, but some parks have overnight accommodation. In Britain, visitors can stay in hotels, youth hostels, campsites and bed and breakfast accommodation in towns and villages. More remote wildernesses usually have a few basic places to stay, such as climbing huts and campsites.

All national parks have a duty to keep people safe. In some African reserves containing dangerous animals, tourists take jeep safaris to view wildlife, but have to stay in the jeep. They sleep in a fenced camp. In North American parks, bears can be a hazard. All visitors are given strict advice not to leave food in the open, where it could attract bears. Even the most remote wildernesses can usually be reached by emergency services such as rescue helicopters if hikers or climbers get into trouble.

Reasons to visit

Recently some of Britain's national parks carried out a survey to find out what drew most people to the park. Spectacular scenery and peace and quiet came top of the list, while some people came to explore attractive villages. Walking was the single most popular activity, with climbing and water sports lower down the list. Visiting shops, cafés and restaurants scored quite low.

DETECTIVE WORK

On a trip to your nearest national park, carry out a survey to find out why people visit. Ask each person you interview to tick one of the following headings: Beautiful scenery, Watching wildlife, Walking, Exploring villages, Visiting shops and cafés, Other activity.

What problems are there for park authorities?

Many national parks receive more and more visitors each year. Park authorities welcome this because it means more people are experiencing the outdoors, and also more money is coming in for conservation and local businesses. However, large numbers of visitors can bring problems such as pollution, litter and overcrowding.

Fuji-Hakone-Izu National Park in Japan is the most popular national park in the world, receiving about 100 million visitors a year. Top attractions include the snow-capped Mount Fuji.

Since the late 1990s, many national parks have attracted record numbers of visitors. Tourist figures have increased partly because people have more leisure time now, and also as car ownership has gone up. Over 90 per cent of visitors to Britain's national parks arrive by car. However cars produce problems. Heavy traffic clogs park roads, especially at peak times. Vehicle exhausts **pollute** the air and traffic noise destroys the peace. In towns and villages, parking can be a problem. All this affects local people as well as visitors.

DETECTIVE WORK

Investigate visitor numbers to Fuji-Hakone-Izu by logging onto the park website using a search engine. If possible, find out how the number of visitors has risen over recent years, and record the results on a chart.

Overcrowding can harm the scenic places that people come to see. Footpaths and **bridleways** can be eroded by hikers' feet, horses' hooves and the wheels of cyclists. Park wardens may have to divert paths to allow worn areas to regrow, or lay stone paths which erode much more slowly. Litter is a problem in national parks worldwide. Drinks cans, tissues and empty bottles are a common sight along many busy trails. In some parks, wardens organise volunteers to clean up litter.

FOCUS ON

Honeypots

The English Lake District is one of Britain's most popular national parks, receiving over 20 million visitors a year. Some of the most attractive villages here, such as Ambleside and Keswick are in danger of being swamped by tourists during the holiday season. Scenic places that are in danger of being spoiled by overcrowding are known as **honeypots**.

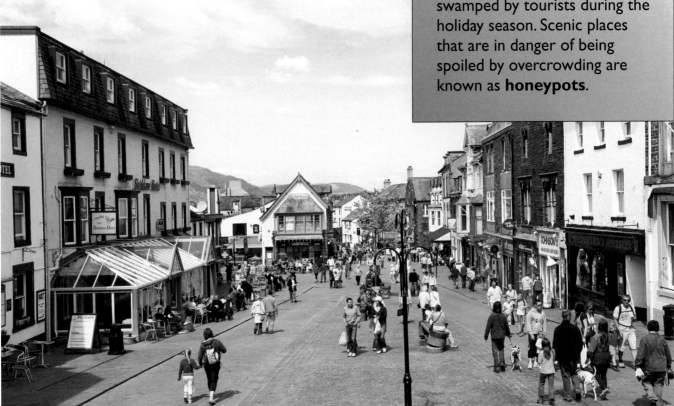

Shops and cafés in Keswick get very crowded at peak holiday times.

Large numbers of visitors can cause conflict with local people. For example, farmers complain that hikers trample crops or break down walls, and that their dogs worry sheep. Local people may find they are unable to afford to buy a home if the demand for holiday cottages makes house prices rise quickly.

Why do you think attractive, overcrowded villages are known as honeypots?

What is the future of national parks and conservation areas?

As the world's population grows, so there is increasing pressure on land for housing, farming and industry. National parks and conservation areas are becoming ever more important. Park authorities struggle to meet the needs of tourists and local people while protecting the environment.

FOCUS ON

Protected land

The International Union for Conservation of Nature (IUCN) recommends that at least 10 per cent of each country is set aside for conservation. Some countries, such as China, meet the target. Around 14 per cent of China is protected. Greenland has one of the highest proportions of protected land, with 40 per cent protected. Other countries fall short of the target. For example, Egypt has less than 8 per cent.

This volunteer is laying a stone path to reduce erosion in Grand Teton National Park, United States.

Find out what percentage of your country is protected using this website: http://mdgs.un.org/unsd/mdg /SeriesDetail.aspx?srid=616

In many parts of the world, parks and conservation areas are threatened by development plans. For example, the United States government is considering allowing mining in the Arctic National Wildlife Refuge in Alaska. The wildlife of this remote wilderness, such as the caribou, could be at risk. In East Africa there are plans to clear parts of the Mabira Rainforest, one of the few remaining forests there, to grow sugar cane.

Most park authorities try to run the park sustainably. This means managing natural resources so that they are preserved for the future. **Sustainable** forestry means planting trees to replace any that are cut down. Sustainable farming includes not using chemicals that damage food chains. Sustainable tourism means meeting the needs of visitors while protecting the natural world. For example, harmful pollution produced by cars can be reduced by improving public transport and encouraging people to use it.

Some parks manage overcrowding by setting aside wilderness or quiet areas, and accepting that popular sites such as honeypots will be very busy. This has happened in the English Lake District. In Yosemite National Park in western United States, tourism is largely confined to the scenic Yosemite Valley, which has campsites, hotels and restaurants. Over 95 per cent of the rest of park is wilderness which sees few tourists.

Use of private cars is discouraged in Yosemite Valley. People use the free bus service to visit waterfalls and other scenery.

DETECTIVE WORK

Conservation begins at home! Encourage local wildlife by creating a wild corner in your garden or schoolyard. A pile of leaves or logs will shelter creatures such as worms and toads. You could make a mini-pond using an old washing-up bowl, and put out food for the birds.

Your project

If you've been doing detective work throughout the book and answered all of Sherlock's questions, you now know a lot about national parks and conservation areas. You could use the information to produce your own project about parks and conservation.

First you'll need to choose a topic that interests you. You could take one of the following questions as a starting point.

Elephants roam a national park in South Africa.

Topic questions
- Find out as much as possible about a park in another country. How did the landscapes form? What are the main habitats, and what types of wildlife live there? You could design food chains showing the connections between wildlife.
- Find out about tourism in two national parks, one in your own country, the other abroad. How do the park authorities provide for tourists? If you can visit the park, you could interview visitors about their response to the park and its services.
- Find out about all the conservation work that goes on in your chosen park. What problems and conservation issues are there, and how are they being tackled?

A penguin in the ice wilderness of Antarctica.

Two cyclists enjoy the scenery of the Lake District.

• Find out about all the different jobs people do in the park, including running services like the parks buses, and working in farming, forestry and other industries if they exist.

Your local library and the Internet can provide all sorts of information to help you. Try the websites listed on page 31. When you have gathered the information you need, present it in an interesting way. You might like to use one of the ideas below.

Sherlock has produced a project about wildlife and food chains in the world's largest national park, the Northeast Greenland National Park. He has found out that the park contains polar bears, which prey on seals, which feed on fish.

Project presentation
• Make a map of the national park in the middle of a large piece of paper. Stick photos, drawings, lists and charts around the edge showing scenery, wildlife, tourist activities and the work of local people.
• Write about life in the park from the point of view of one or more of the following people: a park warden, farmer, mountain-biker, bird-watcher, wildlife expert, shop-owner.
• Write an article for a travel magazine explaining the attractions of the park. Or imagine you are making a TV documentary about the area. Plan a structure to explain what is special about the area, and make a list of all the people you want to interview.

Glossary

alien species An animal or plant that is brought to an area where they don't belong by people.

bridleway Path that can be used by horse-riders as well as people on foot.

canyon A deep gorge carved by a river.

colony A country or region that is controlled by another country.

conservationists People who do conservation work or support conservation.

crust Earth's outer layer.

development Growth and expansion of industries, businesses and services.

endangered Of living things that are at risk of extinction.

environment The surroundings in which people or wildlife live.

erosion When the rocks at Earth's surface are worn away by wind, water, frost or ice.

extinct When a plant or animal species dies out completely, so that none are left.

fold mountain A mountain formed when the plates of Earth's crust collide, and the land between is forced upwards.

habitat Place where particular types of plants and animals live, such as a desert or coral reef.

habitat loss When a wild place where plants and animals live is taken over or changed by people.

herbivore An animal that eats plants.

honeypots Attractive places that are very popular with visitors, and in danger of becoming overcrowded.

Ice Age A long period when Earth's climate was colder than it is now, when ice covered much of the land.

illegally To do something that is against the law.

mineral A non-living natural substance.

native Of plants, animals and other living things that are naturally found in a particular habitat.

plateau An area of high, flat-topped land.

poacher A hunter who acts against the law.

pollute When harmful materials dirty the air, water or soil.

pollution Any harmful substance that damages the environment.

population The number of people or animals living in an area.

population density The number of people (or animals) living in a certain area such as a square kilometre.

predator An animal that hunts other animals for food.

recreation Leisure time for enjoyment.

settlement Place where people live, such as a village or town.

species A particular type of plant or animal, such as the black rhino.

sustainable Of activities and industries that use resources to meet people's needs today while protecting the same resources for the future.

uplift When the rocks at the Earth's surface are raised up to become hills or mountains.

Answers

Page 8: The initials AONB stand for Area of Outstanding Natural Beauty.

Page 11: Britain's national parks are mostly in the north and west, but the New Forest and the South Downs, soon to become a national park, lie in the south.

Page 13: The Grand Canyon is getting a little deeper each year as the Colorado River continues to wear its bed away.

Page 14: The Peak District National Park has 38,000 people living in 1,437 sq km. 38,000 people divided by 1,437 = 26.4 – over 26 people – to each square kilometre. The Lake District has 42,000 people living in 2,292 sq km which gives 18.3 – just over 18 people – to each square kilometre. So the Peak District is more densely populated.

Page 18: Earthworms and slugs eat plants, and are hunted by shrews.

Page 25: Scenic villages are known as honeypots because they swarm with tourists at peak times just as bees swarm around a honeypot.

Further Information

Further reading
The Great Outdoors by Richard Spilsbury (Heinemann, 2005)
National Parks by Sharon Fear (Dorling Kindersley, 2004)
The Mud Pack: Wildlife by James Parry (National Trust Enterprises, 2002)

Websites
National Parks authorities
Britain: www.nationalparks.gov.uk/aboutus
European Parks Federation: www.europarc.org/home/

US National Park Service: www.nps.gov/
Australia: www.cultureandrecreation.gov.au/
New Zealand: www.doc.govt.nz/

Yellowstone National Park
www.nps.gov/yell/

Conservation organisations
The National Trust: www.nationaltrust.org.uk/main/
The Campaign for National Parks, UK: www.cnp.org.uk/
IUCN: www.iucn.org/
Friends of the Earth: www.foe.co.uk
Greenpeace: www.greenpeace.org
World Wide Fund for Nature (WWF): www.worldwildlife.org
WWF's endangered species page: www.worldwildlife.org/species/index.html

Websites offering information about nature and conservation
Animal Planet:www.animal.discovery.com/
BBC's natural history website: www.bbc.co.uk/sn/
National Geographic magazine: www.nationalgeographic.com/
US Fish and Wildlife Service: www.fws.gov/
US Fish and Wildlife Service Endangered Species Program: www.fws.gov/endangered/www.endangered/

Index

The numbers in **bold** refer to pictures